Dewdrops
In The
Moonlight

Dewdrops In The Moonlight:

A Book of Pagan Prayer

by
Shanddaramon

Dewdrops In The Moonlight:
A Book of Pagan Prayer
by Shanddaramon

First Edition
published by
Astor Press
www.astorpress.com

ISBN: 978-0-6151-4497-9

Produced in the United States of America
The author may be contacted at mail@shanddaramon.com.

Dewdrop,
tiny dewdrop,
glistening in the silvery moonlight:
a tiny crystal in the darkness
that glitters softly.
And yet,
on its sparkling surface,
is the face of the moon
and within
is the whole of the dancing universe.

Table of Contents

Preface

Like tiny dew drops that collect on the morning grass before being dissipated by the approaching dawn, our words of prayer are small pearls of condensed thought and offers of praise that are spoken and then sent out into the cosmic forces of the universe. It is said that a single sound can resonate in the universe for thousands of years. Surely, then, it is best to fill the universe with sounds of praise, adoration, and respect.

As the popularity of Paganism continues to spread throughout the world, there is a greater need to provide words of comfort, aid, and adoration for our own particular faith. There will always be occasions when poignant words are needed. These needs may arise when there is neither time nor opportunity to enact a full ritual. Sometimes, we just need a simple prayer - one that emphasizes our own spiritual traditions. Though it is perfectly fitting to speak directly from the heart and improvise your own prayers, for these are often the strongest of prayers, there may come a time when the words simply do not come. By providing a book of prayer for the Pagan community, we can have prayers available for which we can reference our own thoughts. I offer these prayers to you for that purpose: to provide some suggestions of words when they might be needed in the occurrences of everyday life; to offer words of comfort and guidance to those who may need it; to provide words that may help to create working chants for rituals; to provide prayers for those who are not Pagan but who may be called upon, for whatever reason, to speak a Pagan prayer; to help provide words to celebrate the cycles of the Earth and the passages of life; and to help offer thoughts that may help one make a deeper connection with the Earth, her creatures, and the cosmic forces of life.

This book does not offer an explanation of Paganism as there are already many excellent books on that topic. Instead, it assumes an understanding of the basic concepts of Pagan practice. This understanding is not actually required to enjoy and/or use these prayers. If you are not familiar with the religious concepts behind modern Paganism, you may still feel a resonance with the words in this book when you read them. If you have a feeling that the divine is in all things of this Earth, if you believe that there is a single mysterious source of energy in the universe, if you understand that Spirit can be personally accessed through interfaces we call deities and that the choice of deity or spiritual concept is up to the individual and cannot be prescribed with one viewpoint for all, then you will probably feel quite comfortable with the prayers in this collection.

These words have been developed from years of personal and group activity and come from a particular viewpoint of Paganism from which I practice. But, you should not feel limited by one viewpoint. Modern Paganism does not require that you follow only one set of religious principles. You are free to follow your heart in your own pursuit of spiritual truth and the development of your own practice. Therefore, I do not expect that all people will relate to all the precepts implied in these prayers. Instead, you should feel free to alter these prayers to suit your own personal or group practice. Certain assumptions such as the concepts of the Goddess, the God and a third deity I call The Child is implied. These can be approached in whatever manner best suits you. Though these general terms are used, specific names of deities can be substituted or any of them can be deleted until the prayer reflects the true spiritual essence that is your own. It is one of the greatest strengths of our movement that we accept the idea that each person can have his or her own understanding of the sacred. That is why I have written these prayers - so that they can be easily understood or transformed to suit those individual practices.

Dewdrops In The Moonlight

Chapter One

Some Thoughts About Prayer

Why Pray?

Many Pagans are adverse to the idea of prayer because it reminds them of the sort of activity they may have once had to do as a child within another religion. But prayer is more than asking for favors. Prayer is communication with the divine. Many Pagans call themselves panentheists meaning that they believe the divine is both immanent (within all things) and transcendent (beyond all things). Transcendent prayer may, at first, resemble that of the child asking God for great Christmas presents. It is a communication directed to a greater entity beyond the self. As Pagans, however, we recognize that people have different concepts of that greater deity. Whether one believes divinity is a concept or a real entity, prayer allows us to make a connection to the divine. In effect, we can plug ourselves into the currents of the cosmos allowing us to turn that energy on and enlighten us. When we are connected with the universe and the gods, we can more clearly see our path in life. We can clearly see how we need to strengthen ourselves and help others.

Immanent prayer allows us to reach within and see that we are an equal part of the whole fabric of the universe. We seek not so much to ask another entity for help as we attempt to find the strength and energy within ourselves to complete the task at hand. When we feel and honor our own divinity through prayer, we gain a new and expanded concept of the self and we enjoin ourselves with others in our search for universal answers to our challenges in life. Panentheistic prayer communicates to the deity that is within and beyond the individual. We entrain ourselves with the universe and learn to take an active role in the mission of the gods. We learn that what is true for the world is true for the individual. We learn what is meant by "as above, so below."

Another reason to pray is that it is a simple and direct way to turn any activity into a sacred event. By simply reciting a memorized or impromptu prayer, whether aloud or silently, we are instantly reminded that any act can be sacred. Prayer can remind us to be thankful, to recognize sacredness in all people and all things, to honor our deities and each other, or to just set a more peaceful and sanctified tone to activities and events.

Why A Book of Pagan Prayer?

It is said that the best prayers come from the heart. While it is true that prayer created on-the-spot will certainly reflect the true inner thoughts of the supplicant, it is also true that some of us simply do not possess the ability (or the courage) to instantly create a prayer - especially if we are called upon to do so within a group of people. It helps to have a set of prayers on hand. That is the purpose of this collection. Secondly, it helps to have a source of material from which to draw from for inspiration in case you are called upon to create your own prayers. I hope this collection will give you some basis for creating your own prayers that reflect your own traditions and beliefs. Thirdly, there may be those ministers (such as chaplains, interdenominational ministers, etc.) who are not Pagan but who may be called upon to provide words for Pagan prayers and services. This collection can be a valuable resource for all of these situations.

Types of Prayer

There are many ways in which a person can communicate with the universe. The most common is the intercessory prayer. With this prayer, the supplicant (the one doing the praying) is asking a divine presence to intercede or interrupt the normal proceedings of life in order to make a desired change. With intercessory prayer, there is an assumption that there is a greater power beyond us which can act on our behalf. As mentioned earlier, this is the philosophy behind the transcendent god. Since part of the Pagan religion accepts the concept of the transcendental deity, we, too, may use intercessory prayer. But it is not the only type of prayer we may choose to use to connect to our deities. Two other common types of prayer are those for offering gratitude and for the celebration of divine, earthly, and life events. These prayers are for offering something back to the deity that has provided. Whether it is the gods, the Earth, or the energy of the human spirit, the religious person recognizes that he or she is not the agent that causes all events. When something significant happens, we can offer thanks or seek to recognize that significance. By praying in this way, we appreciate the gifts we are given and hope that they will continue.

There are also types of prayers which differ from the image of speaking softly to the gods. These variations include chants or incantations, vows, litanies, and mantras. Chants or incantations are prayers that are usually spoken out loud and are often repeated. Pagans believe in the power of the self to raise energy and to send that energy toward a directed goal. Chants, along with singing, dancing, and drumming, are effective ways in which one can access and increase that energy. Repeated chants, especially with others, allow you to use your voice to reach into the internal vibrations of your body in the same way that we know a car engine is gaining power as its sound becomes louder and fuller. Vows are special promises we make to ourselves, to others, or to our gods. These types of prayers are not to be taken lightly. It is believed that sounds carry into space and exist for thousands of years. If we utter things in a vow we do not actually intend to do, those false words will exist for many years - maybe even lifetimes. Litanies are prayers usually done within a group. They include a single line of words that is repeated by the group interspersed between lines of a prayer offered by the group leader. They are an effective way of encouraging group participation in a prayer. Mantra is a word borrowed from the Buddhist tradition and refers to a word or phrase repeated many times. The mantra can be recited aloud but it is usually recited silently inward. It has a different purpose than the chant. It is not meant to raise energy. Instead, the repeated sound is used to quiet the mind and focus it away from the usually scattered thoughts of everyday living. The mantra is a form of prayer that helps us connect to our inner selves or the part of divinity that is deep within us waiting to be heard as soon as we can quiet our minds and listen.

The Premise of these Prayers

Every prayer has within its words assumptions about the spiritual practice of the supplicant. These prayers are no different. That is why I encourage you to adopt them to suit your own personal theological understanding. However, it helps to understand the assumptions embedded within the prayers in this collection before reading or using the prayers for yourself. The prayers within this book are based upon the assumption that there exists a single source of all existence which I call Spirit. I believe that this source cannot be truly known by mortals and, so, we must relate to it through two forces which emanate from it. These two forces are complementary opposites and we relate to them best in terms of the duality of male and female. I call them the Goddess and the God. Pagans may honor and worship these two entities as Goddess and God or through a variety of deities from long existing or newly created pantheons. A list of traditional pantheons is given at the end of this book. I have not used any of the traditional names from the pantheons allowing you to add those names as you wish.

The next assumption used in these prayers is that the energies of the gods have no purpose or meaning if there is not a manifestation through which they can exist. This reality is honored through a deity known in my tradition as the Child. With the Goddess, the God, and the Child, a sacred trinity is completed. The concept of the trinity is sacred in many religions because it represents a balance of forces through manifestation and change. Most of us are aware of the Christian trinity of the Father, the Son, and the Holy Ghost which may have been derived from the gnostic trinity of God, Jesus, and Sophia. In Buddhism, there is the Sangha (priesthood), the Buddha (the prophet), and the Dharma (the laws). Islam recognizes God, the prophet Mohammed, and the Koran as its trinity. Taoism speaks of the Tao (the source), the Way, and the Chi (life force) as the three essential elements of its theology. Plato spoke of goodness, truth, and beauty as the great trinity of the philosopher. The number three is known as equally significant in Celtic religions as well.

The prayers also assume that the three deities represent or, if you will, are the faces of three cosmic energies. The God is the source of Light - not just the light we see in the sun or from the household light bulb but the light that is the life force in all things. Both the Buddha (Be ye a lamp unto yourselves) and Jesus (Yet a little while is the light with you. Walk while ye have the light, lest darkness come upon you: for he that walketh in darkness knoweth not whither he goeth.) spoke of the need to let your inner light shine through. Light is what gives us the desire to be separate individuals. It is the source of our need to create and be noticed. The Goddess is the source of Love.

Again, I am speaking about more than the love of your favorite pet or your lover. I am talking about the love that binds the universe together - the strength of unity that keeps us from spinning out of control. Love is the force that bonds us to each other. It is the source of our need to be with others and to nurture and protect. The Child is the recognition that all of life is equally sacred to the God and Goddess. It is the midpoint between expanding and returning. It is the source of where we can find peace and joy in our own lives. I have limited these prayers to only using these three concepts making it easy for you to transform them to your own needs.

Writing Your Own Prayers

The process of writing your own prayers is similar to the process of writing any other creative project except that it involves the inclusion of your deities in the considerations. The easiest way to write your own prayers is to simply use the ones in this collection and alter the words or names to suit your own purposes. There may come a time, though, when you feel the need to create your own prayers. Before doing this, make sure you have a clear understanding of your theology. To whom or what are you praying and why are good questions to ask yourself. Other questions you might ask yourself include: "What type of prayer am I trying to write?" "What do I hope to have happen or what do I wish to honor?" "Where and when will this prayer take place?" "Is it meant for a group or just myself?" Then, in a few words, write out the essence of the prayer. Next, you might want to meditate or enact a ritual and ask that the right words be given to you. If you listen quietly and patiently, the words will come.

Most standard prayers have four parts to them: 1) the invocation, 2) the listing, 3) the request, and 4) the closing. The invocation is the calling of the name of the deity. It is the time when you ask him or her to be present. Next is a listing of the attributes, qualities or achievements of the deity - especially those related to the purpose of the prayer. After that would come the actual request. This may come in the form of a request for a service, it may be a request for a blessing, or may be simply a request to be present and witness an occasion. This is followed by a simple closing word or phrase. Many religious traditions use the same basic closing for each prayer signaling a ritualistic ending. The word "Amen" serves that purpose well in the Christian tradition. An example of this format might look like:

invocation:	O Ancient gods, I call to you.
listing:	You who have blessed the daysof my life,
request:	Come now again to witness the dedication of this child into the path of your ways.
closing:	For the good of one and all, so mote it be.

How To Pray

We all know the traditional method of prayer where the supplicant is on his or her knees, hands cupped in front, and head down. This, of course, is only one of many ways in which to pray. Assuming a particular body position can have a role in engaging in effective prayer. If the only time you get on your knees with folded hands is to pray to your deity, then your mind and body take that position to be a symbol and form for that activity exclusively. The body position becomes a trigger for you. When you take on that position your mind instantly thinks "It's time now to pray." You switch from thinking and feeling about everyday concerns and instantly begin to prepare for prayer. It may help to find a body position suitable for creating such a trigger within yourself but it is not necessary. What is important is how you approach prayer. You must prepare all the parts of yourself - your body, your mind, your heart and your soul. Your body must be in a place where it will not be disturbed, the mind must be focused, the heart must be open, and the soul must be connected to your deities. Pagans believe that any space can be sacred. By creating either physically or mentally a circle around yourself you are claiming that spot to be the center of the world and, therefore, sacred. Your mind should be focused on your goal. This is what we mean by intent. All sacred acts must be underscored by an intent. This intent must be carefully examined and considered to be right and truly necessary before it can be applied. From then on, the intent is the focus behind all the words spoken in the prayer. The heart must be open. Prayers to the universe cannot be clouded with hate or anger. This would be like offering your best friend a rotten apple. The mind must be free of prejudices so that it can be open and receptive to what the gods may offer in return for your words. Finally, the soul - the spark of the divine within yourself - must be connected to your deities. Not doing so would be like trying to call someone without first picking up the phone. Our cell phone to the universe is the soul and we need to sense that we are connected before beginning the call.

Dewdrops In The Moonlight

Chapter Two

Wiccan Prayers

The first two writings in this collection have been called the traditional words for Wiccans. They are seen in almost all Wiccan texts and are mentioned as being the main guiding principles in Wiccan practice. The next two prayers in this collection are from ethical principles used in the Sacred Order of Living Paganism – the group of which I am a member. Individuals in our tradition are expected not to take the words to heart without personally exploring whether they are true and right for that person. I invite you to do the same and change or alter these prayers and principles to suit your personal understanding of that which is the right way for you to live a spiritual life. We would say, that as long as your personal ethics do not violate the principle of "no harm" expressed in the Rede, than it is true and correct for you.

The Wiccan Rede

Bide the Wiccan Law Ye must
In Perfect Love and in Perfect Trust.
Nine words the Wiccan Rede fulfill
An' as it harm none, do what Ye will.
What Ye sends forth comes back to thee.
So ever mind the Rule of Three.
Thus, bright the cheek and warm the heart
As Merry Ye Meet and Merry Ye Part.

The Rule of Three

Remember the Rule of Three is true
that which you send returns threefold to you
This lesson well, you must know
You shall only receive that which you let flow!

A Statement of Belief
(The Thirteen Principles
of the Order)

With true mind and heart do I hereby state that I believe:

1) in a single mysterious source of all existence.
2) in the division of the one source into two equal and complimentary entities whom I call the Goddess and the God and whom I honor through my own deities.
3) in honoring, respecting, and revering the source of all by celebrating the cycles of Nature through joyous ritual.
4) that the cycles of Nature teach me about the cycles of life including the cycle of life and death. Therefore, I believe that life can be renewed through Spirit, that I can learn from the experiences of the past and that what I do now affects the future lives of myself and others.
5) that the physical world is not the only reality and that other realms may be explored and engaged.
6) in the power to focus and direct the will in order to enact transformations for the good of the self and all others.
7) in free will which requires me to understand the responsibilities inherent in acting in accordance with this freedom.
8) that good and evil are the result of the consequences of free will. Thus, I seek to act and lead my life in ways which, to the greatest degree possible, do not cause harm to myself or others.
9) in the application of ethical principles such as the Wiccan Rede, the Threefold Law and the Five Precepts to my daily life.
10) that all sacred paths and practices which do not cause harm to others are worthy of toleration and respect and that I can learn and grow from the wisdom of the world's religious traditions and philosophies.
11) that spiritual truth can be sought in modern as well as ancient knowledge; that the theories of quantum physics and Jungian psychology are as inspiring as the ancient mysteries and the ways of magick.
12) in celebrating the solstices, equinoxes and cross quarter days

(sabbats) in public ritual, the full moons (esbats) in small group ritual, and the dark moons (astors) in personal ritual.

13) that each person has the ability and right to become a member of the clergy and that no single person has the right to dominate the spiritual life of another.

A Code of Conduct
(the Five Precepts
of the Order)

To the best of my ability and through all intent, I vow to live my life
through the principles of:
1. **Reverence**: I will live as I will to my full potential - without
   causing harm to myself, to others, or to Earth.
2. **Respect**: I will promote and honor all others who seek no
   harm.
3. **Reason**: I will live not by the rule of others but by the right
   intent of myself.
4. **Responsibility**: I will live in joy knowing that what is sent is
   also returned.
5. **Revelry**: I will live and act always with joy and honor.

Common Prayers

These prayers are designed for common everyday events. The first prayer is to offer thanks. We may often pray or do rituals and then forget to thank the universe for our good fortune. We may mistakenly believe that we are the ones who made the event of which we requested come to pass. Since we believe that we are part of the divine, it is right to think that our efforts played a part in the manifestation of our desires but we also believe that the whole of divinity is greater than the individual and must remember that we can do nothing on our own. It is right, then, to offer thanks whenever something goes our way or which my help to make the world a better place in which to live.

Remaining prayers in this section are directed toward other feelings associated with living in the divine presence of Eternal Spirit. Each helps us to find the proper mindset needed to accept the tasks at hand.

Giving Thanks

O great Goddess of Love
I thank you for the gift of loving
and of being worth the love of others.
I thank you for beauty and wonder
and for the chance to be in awe.
I thank you for the love of others
and for the chance to be together.
I thank you for the love of the divine
and for the chance to be within it
in this life and in all.

O Great God of Light,
I thank you for the gift of living
and of sharing it with others.
I thank you for knowledge and wisdom
and for the chance to learn.
I thank you for strength and guidance
and for the chance to become who I am.
I thank you for life and laughter
and for the chance to know joy.

Before Meditation

Spirit of the universe,
from both within and beyond,
by which we know as God and Goddess,
we seek to know and experience
your wisdom and beauty through
this act of worship and prayer we call meditation.
Help us to see beyond the dark veil of separateness
into the light of unity.
Help us to learn, grow, and be filled with your wisdom and love.

Compassion

O Lady of unending love,
teach me compassion
that I may help to make the world stronger
through understanding and love.
I wish to do this for others
as I wish to do this for myself,
for compassion is the bond of living.
Give me the strength and courage
to walk the path of compassion.

Perseverance

O Lord and Lady
O Child of wonder,
give me the strength
to continue to walk the path
to your knowledge, love and understanding.
I know the path is long and winding.
I know that it will be full of challenges,
but such is the path of truth and freedom
for I do not follow the blind course of others.
I follow yours which is also mine.
I have chosen this way of my own free will.
As I honor the gods from within and beyond,
let that praise become my beacon of guidance
as I continue ever forward.

Patience

O God of Light,
as you are patient in bringing your light to the world,
teach me patience.
O Goddess of Love,
as you are patient in bringing us together,
teach me patience.
O Child of Life,
as you are patient in returning to the Spirit,
teach me patience.

Patience II

O Gods of infinite patience
who have been here from the first
and shall remain to the end,
gently guiding us to greater wisdom and compassion,
bless me with the strength and love
of patience.
Let me act not in anger
but in temperance.

Faith

Great Gods of ancient times,
I call upon you
to give me the faith I need
to carry on in your name.
As a student of your mysteries,
I know that I cannot know all things
but I know that I can believe.
Show me the way to see what cannot be seen.
Open up my mind's eye.
Let me be strong in my convictions
for I shall follow my heart
where you shall lead it.
Open my mind, fill me with love,
speak to me in your silent whispers,
show me truth in the ways of your children.
If I can do these things
and act with good intent
in all that I do,
I know I shall be filled with your blessings
and shall live in faith.

Hope

O Sweet Goddess,
with you I can remain hopeful
for yours is the unending love
of all things and all times.
O Strong God,
with you I can remain hopeful
for yours is the unending fortitude
needed to always carry on.
O Gentle Child,
with you I can remain hopeful
for yours is the dark mystery
from which all answers can be sought.
Gods of the unending power of hopefulness,
give me hope,

Love

O Great Goddess of Love.
You have shown me how love
is important in my life and the lives of others.
Let me hold fast to this truth.
Let me learn to love myself and to extend that love
to those beyond me.
For love is the binder of all things.
Teach me to recognize when I stray
from the teachings of love
and show me how to find my way back to you.
Teach me love that knows no limits.
Show me how to give love as well as receive it.
Thus, I will be blessed by you for all of my days.

Stress

O Sacred Child of Life
It is to you I call in these times of stress.
You are the secret mystery of Life.
You are the silence in the center of the turning wheel.
Teach me to hear the silence.
Teach me to be still and calm.
Let me think of you and only you
so that my mind my find its center.
Let me relax my body.
Let me unwind my emotions.
Let me unravel the bonds about my soul.
Like a great ocean,
show me how to still the waters,
wave by ever slowing wave,
until they become ripples
and simple undulations
until the waters are calmed.

Fear

O Great God of strength,
I see the boldness of your fortitude
shining in the brightness of the sun.
Give me the same strength to face my fears.
Show me how to unshackle the bonds of my worries.
Give me clear insight to see beyond this wall I face
to the other side.
Fill me with your power until I know
that I can take on this fear.
Show me the causes of my fear
so I may uproot them like weeds
and toss them aside
until my field of vision is clear
and I may move forward, ever forward
with the strength of your light within.

Daily Prayers

Daily prayers keep us connected on a regular basis to our practice, our deities, and to the universe. Like almost any activity, we must have a regular practice in order to stay connected with our spiritual understanding and our with our relationship to that which we worship. It is a chance to remind ourselves of who we really are and from where we can truly derive our strength. There are too many reminders of the need to satisfy the personal ego and too few practices that remind us that we are part of something greater than ourselves.

Meditation

O good powers of light here be
in clear mind I beckon thee.
Grant me mystic knowing pure.
Let inner peace and joy endure.
Let through me your work befall
for the aid and betterment of all.
Clear the way for my mind to see
the truth of knowing what is within me.

Daily Chant I

I offer praises to this day most divine
for all days are sacred when I incline
to feel the presence of the gods
and to live in the blessing of the gods.
For I abide in them as they abide in me
and to live in this way is to live most sacredly.

Daily Chant II

Sacred altar I honor thee
and to all thy agents, blessed be.
Let this day be just as holy
and may I come to live it fully.

At Dawn

I offer praises to the bringer of the golden dawn
whose light pierces the darkness;
whose heat warms the cold heart.
You, who give birth to the new day
and let life continue on in its pursuit of joy and beauty
Illumine me, warm me, enlighten me.

Morning I

I sing praise to the morning sun,
O bright and glorious one!
Provider of warmth, of light, of heat;
Great fire of the East that makes life complete.
Symbol of God, of strength, and wisdom true,
I take this time to humbly honor you.

Morning II

As the morning sun begins to rise,
let the beauty of this day fill my eyes.
As I start this day most sacred,
let me find no need for hatred.
Let me, instead, create and seek
those moments of joy that make life unique.

Noon

Lord of light,
who blazes in the height of the heavens;
who sits in the high throne of the day;
who has made this day bright and glorious;
who has brought warmth
and given us the chance to grow,
I offer my praise and thanks to you.

Dusk

Hail to you great Sun,
riding your blazing chariot beyond the horizon;
offering us again a dazzling display of your glory;
teach me to know my own endings with such honor.
Let me take this time to recall what joys have filled me this day.
Show me how to face the darkness without despair
and grant me safe sleep until I can rise with you again.

Evening

I am thankful to be
most fully alive and healthy
and I am thankful for the chance
to live yet one more day
in which I can be joyful
in all I do and say.

Bedtime

O gods and goddesses of the earth and sky,
O great mysterious force of life,
grant me this time of rest and peace.
Let me take stock of my day
and be glad for it.
May it also be this way for others
when they go to rest.
Grant peace and comfort to all those in this place.
Grant peace and comfort to all those in this community.
Grant peace and comfort to all beings everywhere
so that we may rise in a better world for one and all.

For Dreamwork

I call on you
beautiful Goddess –
you who holds the chalice of dreams.
As I prepare myself now for sleep,
let me be conscious of my trip
across your waters between wake and sleep.
Give me clear vision to see the dreams to come.
Give me this time to learn your lessons
in the images that you impart to me.
Part the veil of imagination
and send me in full view
to that time of endless time,
that place of forever vision.
Teach me to interpret the dreamscape I shall encounter
and show me how to use what I learn for good and right.
With your blessing,
send me off to that sleep of wonders.

At Night With a Moon

O great and beautiful Goddess,
whose light shines down in silver threads,
teach me to appreciate the quietness.
Teach me to appreciate the small things
which are so great.
Teach me to better love myself
and all beings.
Teach me to honor you in all my work
and in all my relationships
and in this way
may I truly worship you.

At Night Without a Moon

O great and silent mystery
that is the core of all life,
teach me to embrace the dark.
Show me how to live in the unknown.
Let me know the wonder of the many stars
that shine down upon me.
Through these things may I come to know and honor you.

This Moment Now

May I always remember:
This time is as sacred as any myth.
This place is as sacred as any temple.
This body is as sacred as any deity.
This mind is as sacred as any tome.
This soul is as sacred as any breath.
This life is as sacred as any light.
Let it be so for all times and all places
and for all manifestations.

Prayers for Group Work

Even solitary practitioners seek times to join with others to celebrate and honor the gods and one another. We are a social being. By practicing with others, we can begin to see hints of the totality of Spirit. By practicing and discussing with others of similar spiritual philosophies, we can gain strength in support of one another. The Greeting and Parting are simple prayers offered from one person to another. It reminds us to recognize that we are all part of the divine. The Bow has a similar purpose but is a more formal version of the Parting and is often done at the end of events and rituals. Other prayers in this section are designed for different types of gatherings such as meetings and events where a group prayer is needed. The Prayer of Tolerance was designed specifically for interfaith meetings and is meant to speak in broad terms in order to help others find unity with pagan belief. The Litany of Praise was designed with a pagan gathering in mind where those attending can agree to similar religious concepts and do not object to responding as a group to the statements.

Greeting

Within you I recognize the light of the God
and the love of the Goddess.
O Child of the divine,
I greet you.

Parting

From mind, heart, body, and soul,
may you in love and peace go.
And from Spirit from which we all came,
merry meet, merry part and merry meet again.

Bow
(the Parting with motions)

(place hands together)
From mind (touch forehead), heart (touch chest),
body (open hands, cross arms and touch shoulders),
and soul (uncross arms and bring forward with palms up),
may you in love and peace go.
And from Spirit from which we all came (place hands together again),
merry meet, merry part and merry meet again (bring hands in and
bow).

Gatherings

O God and Goddess,
O deities of many names,
O light and love of life,
we gather here in your presence
to honor and worship you
as we seek to honor and worship ourselves.
For we know we are of the gods and yet
are only a spark of the eternal spirit.
May we come together in this understanding
and with the same honor, respect, and love for each other
that we hope and seek from you.

Meetings

Lord of Light and Lady of Love,
be with us and bless us as we here gather together.
Guide us to do what is right
and not just convenient.
Guide us to seek the truth
and not just the comforting.
Guide us to do what is needed
and not just the easy.
Guide us to do the necessary
and not just the desired.
Guide us to be fair
in all our dealings
and to be just.
Guide us to be true to our actions
and not just large in our words.
Guide us to be gentle
to the Earth, our mother
and to ourselves and to each other.

Religious Tolerance

O Spirit of Life, whom we know through so many names,
O great unknown, whom we seek through many sources,
as you are tolerant of all life which is your creation and your existence
teach us also to be tolerant of all ways of praising you.
For all acts of good and right are sacred
and all thoughts of truth and justice are sacred.
Teach us and remind us that
we are all but small parts of an infinite greater whole
which is ultimate truth and righteousness for all beings.

Litany of Praise

To all gods and all goddesses
of all names and traditions,
we offer praise.
To all spirits of all places and practices,
we offer praise.
For all people of all races
and all creeds and of all persuasions
who work for the good of one and all,
we offer praise.
For all these powers of goodness and justice,
we offer praise.
To the spirits of the East
who bring wisdom and sharing,
we offer praise.
To the spirits of the South
who bring energy and light,
we offer praise.
To the spirits of the West
who bring understanding and cooperation,
we offer praise.
To the Spirits of the North
who bring us the chance to be with one another
in joy and peace,
we offer praise.
To all those present in mind, heart, soul, body and in spirit,
we offer praise.

Family Gathering

O Ancient Ones,
We gather here as a family
to share with one another
as a reflection of the Great Family:
Goddess, God and Child.
As with you,
let us now come together
to support one another.
Let the qualities of one
be the strength for another.
Let us find balance in the uniqueness
of each other.
Let us speak and act with honesty and dignity
and let us find the same in each other.
Let us practice to be what we seek the world to be.
Let us represent the ideals of our spiritual path
as we walk that path together
as family.

Dewdrops In The Moonlight

Chapter Three

Chants for Ritual

This section offers chants that can be used within the many parts of a magick ritual. They can be viewed as prayers or as chants for ritual work. They are offered here in the order of a typical Pagan ritual format. One of the first and most important parts of any ritual is the Statement of Intention. It is through your intent that all other activities of the ritual will flow and it is your intent which you hope to offer to the universe in order to seek help. Your intent must be carefully thought out and speaking it aloud helps to clarify and solidify your purpose. The Banishing helps to clear away any ill intent which may exist in the place where you are working.

The next step in ritual design is to purify your working space. With the Purification chant, the area is purified through the four elements. Next, a circle is cast and the four directions are recognized. Then, a circle of protection is cast. The next steps are to invoke the quarters, your deities, and the two layers (above and below) into your circle. After completing the circle, enact your ritual and then undo the circle in the opposite order of invocation. An additional chant is provided here for creating a portal in your circle for those times when you forgot to turn off the coffee machine after creating your circle.

Statement of Intention

It is I, [ritual name] who come before thee to initiate this circle of power for the purpose I state: [state purpose, light candle of intent]

Banishing

If any ill intent here be, by these sounds I banish thee.

Purification

By Fire and Air, I sanctify. By Water and Earth, I purify. By the powers of the God and Goddess, I claim this sacred space and hallow it now as my special place.

Casting a Circle

In this circle now I spin, a sacred rite shall soon begin.
May I now be safe and sure for the work I here procure.

Calling in the Quadrants

Guardians of the East, element of Air, realm of the mind, direction of the rising sun and new beginnings, I call to you.

Guardians of the South, element of Fire, realm of the heart, direction of the noonday sun and fortitude, I call to you.

Guardians of the West, element of Water, realm of the soul, direction of the setting sun and endings, I call to you.

Guardians of the North, element of Earth, realm of the physical, direction of the dark of night and renewal, I call to you.

Call to the Deities

O Goddess of the Moon, great feminine one,
bless this sacred circle and all work within it done.

O God of the Sun, great masculine one,
bless this sacred circle and all work within it done.

O Child of Center, great mysterious one
bless this sacred circle and all work within it done.

Call to the Layers

O Father Sky above, realm of sun, moon, and stars,
here below I stand in reflection
to ask for your guidance and protection

O Mother Earth below, realm of the four quadrants,
here above I stand in reflection
to ask for your guidance and protection

Closing the Circle

With love and trust shall we hold fast
for now, at last, the circle is cast.

Releasing the Layers

O Mother Earth below, realm of the four quadrants,
here above I stand in reflection to thank you now for your protection

O Father Sky above, realm of sun, moon, and stars,
here below I stand in reflection to thank you now for your protection

Thanking the Deities

O Child of the Stars, great mysterious one,
with you my work here has now been done.
If you have come to bless this rite,
I thank you now for your great light.

O God of the Sun, great masculine one,
with you my work here has now been done.
If you have come to bless this rite,
I thank you now for your great light.

O Goddess of the Moon, great feminine one,
with you my work here has now been done.
If you have come to bless this rite,
I thank you now for your great light.

Releasing the Quadrants

Guardians of the West, depart. To your watery realm impart.
Bless all here gathered in true mind and heart.
Hail and Farewell! Blessed Be!

Guardians of the South, depart. To your fiery realm impart.
Bless all here gathered in true mind and heart.
Hail and Farewell! Blessed Be!

Guardians of the East, depart. To your airy realm impart.
Bless all here gathered in true mind and heart.
Hail and Farewell! Blessed Be!

Guardians of the North, depart. To your earthly realm impart.
Bless all here gathered in true mind and heart.
Hail and Farewell! Blessed Be!

Opening the Circle

Now this circle I undo for the sacred rite is through.
Let these blessings I bestow, like a seed take root and grow.
The circle is open, but its bonds remain unbroken

Opening and Closing A Portal

I open this magick gate.
Let passage no powers dissipate.

I close this magick gate.
Let hence no power abnegate.

Chants For Magick

There are already plenty of books available for writing and enacting spells of all kinds. I offer only a few chants here. More importantly, though, I offer some supportive prayers and chants that can go with spell work.

Re-invoking a spell

To this spell I re-invoke
the powers sought in words once spoke.
To thus fruition bearing when
I speak these hopeful words again.

Offer Gratitude After a Successful Spell

To all the powers here amassed,
I thank thee for what now has past.
For this spell cast in right servitude,
let its energies return with gratitude.
And if in its wake more good can come
let that work yet still be done.

Seeking a Magickal Tool

To do the work of worthy bidding
this request requires fulfilling.
A(n) _____ with magick potent full
is what I seek as my ritual tool.

Consecrating a Magickal Tool

O powers that here congregate,
to righteous work this tool I dedicate.
To it my will and purpose integrate.
This sacred [object] I hereby consecrate.
Fill it with your magic light
so it I may employ for good and right.
and may it with each use invite
greater good and further insight.

Imbuing An Object

Into this [object] I imbue
the power of what hence I do.
Let to its purpose my charge be true
until the magick work is through.

Changing and Consecrating The Altar

Sacred altar,
Realm of visions,
symbol of the integrated being,
the ground beneath our feet,
accept and support
the weight of my intent.
Prepare the way
for good works and offerings
as they are mutually beneficial to all.

Travel Protection

On this day and in this hour
I call upon the higher powers.
Oh you the God of earth and sun,
let my will be ever done.
Oh Goddess of the moon and sea,
ensure that _____ travel safely.
Protect them as they are away
so that they may return someday
and on their journey here and there
let love and kindness follow everywhere.
Keep them safe from any harm.
Hold their spirit in your arms.

Safety

Because there is good,
we know there is evil,
for they are of the same source of living.
And we know it is through our choices
and the consequences of those choices that good and evil exist.
But because there is evil does not mean
that there must also be harm.
I ask that those who do not know
the wisdom of light in the God,
or the wonders of love in the Goddess,
or the joys of life in the Child,
not be allowed to harm,
but instead be shown these truths.

Rain

O Great Sun,
we ask but for a short time
that you hide your face from us
and bring forth a veil of clouds.
O Great Mother Earth,
we ask that you bring forth from those clouds
the life giving water that we call rain
so that life may grow
and all may drink in your splendor.

Seasonal Prayers

The following litanies are designed to be used in group celebrations of the two solstices, the two equinoxes and the days between called cross-quarter days. These are the eight Sabbats of Pagan practice. Following these is a litany for the Esbat or the celebration of the full moon which is usually dedicated to the Goddess. Finally, there is a poem for the Astor or celebration of the Child on the dark moon. In my tradition, Sabbats are public rituals open to all and Esbats are for smaller groups of people all with experience in working with energy while the Astor is a private individual ritual.

Samhain

O Great Goddess, we call to you.
Bless us one and all!
O Great God, we call to you.
Bless us one and all!
O Great Child within, we call to you.
Bless us one and all!
Come to us as we celebrate the apex of Autumn.
Bless us one and all!
Join us in this solemn festival of Samhain.
Bless us one and all!
We honor you in this time of death and endings.
Bless us one and all!
Let us honor those who have come before us.
Bless us one and all!
Let us honor those whose lives have taught and guided us.
Bless us one and all!
Let us continue to fight for justice so none will die in vain.
Bless us one and all!
That our work may bring peace, joy, and love to all in your name.
Bless us one and all!
Bless us, Bless us, Bless us!

Yule

O Great Goddess, we call to you.
Bless us one and all!
O Great God, we call to you.
Bless us one and all!
O Great Child within, we call to you.
Bless us one and all!
Come to us as we celebrate the Winter solstice.
Bless us one and all!
Join us in this sacred festival of Yule.
Bless us one and all!
Let us honor you in this time of rebirth.
Bless us one and all!
Show us how to live in the dark as well as the light.
Bless us one and all!
Show us how to rest and renew ourselves.
Bless us one and all!
Great new sun, we await your arrival.
That our work may bring peace, joy, and love to all in your name.
Bless us one and all!
Bless us, Bless us, Bless us!

Imbolc

O Great Goddess, we call to you.
Bless us one and all!
O Great God, we call to you.
Bless us one and all!
O Great Child within, we call to you.
Bless us one and all!
Come to us as we celebrate the apex of Winter.
Bless us one and all!
Join us in this festival of Imbolc.
Bless us one and all!
We honor you in this time of beginnings and dedications.
Bless us one and all!
We find comfort in the warmth of the festival fire.
Bless us one and all!
We are reminded of these joys in the burning of our candles.
Bless us one and all!
We find comfort in the returning of the light.
Bless us one and all!
and we look forward to the return of the warmth.
Bless us one and all!
That our work may bring peace, joy, and love to all in your name.
Bless us one and all!
Bless us, Bless us, Bless us!

Ostara

O Great Goddess, we call to you.
Bless us one and all!
O Great God, we call to you.
Bless us one and all!
O Great Child within, we call to you.
Bless us one and all!
Come to us as we celebrate the Spring equinox.
Bless us one and all!
Join us in this sacred festival of Ostara.
Bless us one and all!
We honor you in this season of fertility.
Bless us one and all!
Let us plant seeds for growth as you have, great Mother.
Bless us one and all!
Let those seedlings be filled with sunshine, great Father.
Bless us one and all!
Let us be joyful for the beauty of Spring.
Bless us one and all!
Let us take time to see and small the flowers.
Bless us one and all!
Let us once again join with nature.
Bless us one and all!
That our work may bring peace, joy, and love to all in your name.
Bless us one and all!
Bless us, Bless us, Bless us!

Beltane

O Great Goddess, we call to you.
Bless us one and all!
O Great God, we call to you.
Bless us one and all!
O Great Child within, we call to you.
Bless us one and all!
Come to us as celebrate the height of Spring.
Bless us one and all!
Join us in this sacred festival of Beltane.
Bless us one and all!
We honor you in this time of your sacred marriage.
Bless us one and all!
We thank you for the beauty and wonder that has surrounded us.
Bless us one and all!
and we look forward to the joys of summer.
Bless us one and all!
That our work may bring peace, joy, and love to all in your name.
Bless us one and all!
Bless us, Bless us, Bless us!

Litha

O Great Goddess, we call to you.
Bless us one and all!
O Great God, we call to you.
Bless us one and all!
O Great Child within, we call to you.
Bless us one and all!
Come to us as we celebrate the Summer solstice.
Bless us one and all!
Join us in this sacred festival of Litha.
Bless us one and all!
We honor you in this time of sacred union and sensuality.
Bless us one and all!
We thank you for this time of great warmth and light.
Bless us one and all!
We thank you for the chance to commune with you.
Bless us one and all!
That our work may bring peace, joy, and love to all in your name.
Bless us one and all!
Bless us, Bless us, Bless us!

Lammas

O Great Goddess, we call to you.
Bless us one and all!
O Great God, we call to you.
Bless us one and all!
O Great Child within, we call to you.
Bless us one and all!
Come to us as we celebrate the height of summer.
Bless us one and all!
Join us in this sacred festival of Lammas.
Bless us one and all!
We honor you in this time of harvest.
Bless us one and all!
Help us to gather in our own crops.
Bless us one and all!
Help us to be mindful of what we have done.
Bless us one and all!
That our work may bring peace, joy, and love to all in your name.
Bless us one and all!
Bless us, Bless us, Bless us

Mabon

O Great Goddess, we call to you.
Bless us one and all!
O Great God, we call to you.
Bless us one and all!
O Great Child within, we call to you.
Bless us one and all!
Come to us as we celebrate the Autumn equinox.
Bless us one and all!
Join us in this sacred festival of Mabon.
Bless us one and all!
We honor you in this time of harvest bounty.
Bless us one and all!
Help us to be thankful for our joys and gifts.
Bless us one and all!
Help us to honor and praise those who have helped us.
Bless us one and all!
Let us honor and praise you for providing for us.
Bless us one and all!
That our work may bring peace, joy, and love to all in your name.
Bless us one and all!
Bless us, Bless us, Bless us

Litany for the Esbat

O Great Goddess,
we call to you.
you whose face we see in the silvery moonlight,
we call to you.
you whose love we feel in the dark of night,
we call to you.
you who comes to us in dreams and visions,
we call to you.
you who speaks to us in our divinations
we call to you.
you who brings forth new life on this green earth,
we call to you.
you who teaches us about birth, death, and rebirth
we call to you.
Join us in this sacred esbat.
we call to you.
We honor you on this sacred night.
we call to you.
Show us the way to your wisdom.
we call to you.
Show us the way to love all creatures and all things.
we call to you.
Help us to hear your message.
we call to you.
Let us honor and praise you now.
we call to you.
That our work may bring peace, joy, and love to all in your name.
we call to you.

Prayer for the Astor

O Great Child,
fill me with the fullness of life.
Teach me to appreciate this precious gift.
Show me how not to fear the night.
Show me how not to fear the unknown.
Show me how to embrace change.
Show me how to live in the mystery
without always seeking answers.
Show me how to be a shining star in the darkness.
Teach me to seek hope and not despair.
I honor you on this sacred starlit night.
Let me honor and praise you now.
That my work may bring peace, joy, and love all in your name.

Prayers for Life Events

Life is full of wonderfully exciting events that change our lives.
These are major points in our journeys and need to be honored and
recognized. We can view them as gifts from the gods and, so, we take
the opportunities to enjoy these milestones while also thanking the
gods for these sacred presents.

Sacred Unions

That there might be love for us,
the Goddess gave us a spark of eternal love.
That there might be energy
through which we can know this love,
the God gave us a spark of eternal light.
That this love might be manifest
so that this love could be shared,
there came the Child –
the sacred and mysterious gift of life.
Love of the self creates inner peace.
Love of another creates joy.
Love of many others creates community.
Love of all beings creates greater peace.
Through love, with love, and in love
we praise and worship
the Ancient Ones, the world, and ourselves
and as one grain of sand reveals the entire universe,
so this one union reveals the beauty of all love.

A Wedding Vow

In the presence of the Goddess,
who is the source and ideal of all love,
in the presence of the God who has made us unique
so that we may support one another,
in the name of the sacred Child,
who makes it possible for us to be as one,
and in witness of these people,
I take you to be my wedded partner, my friend, my lover, and my companion.
I vow to share both the brightness and the darkness that life may bring our way.
I vow to give and receive, to share and listen, to love, support, and challenge you.
I vow to share my hopes and my dreams.
I vow to provide support and respect to you always
From this day forward.

Pregnancy

O Ancient Great Ones,
the miracle of birth
which is your greatest gift
is upon us.
Give us strength
in this time of waiting and nurturing.
Let us all be of good health.
Give this child what it needs to grow and live
so that through its presence,
(a manifestation of the mystery)
we can truly honor you and praise you.

Birth

As we honor the dawning of the sun in the morning,
as we honor the waxing of the silver moon,
as we honor the rebirth of flowers in the spring,
so we honor this birth of a new child.
Bless this little one
so that it may grow strong, wise and full of love;
so that it may worship you as we do -
each in our own ways.

For the Dying

Gentle Goddess,
you have taught us about the cycles of life
and of the gifts of rebirth.
We know now that this soul must depart
and return to you.
We are saddened by our loss
but take joy in knowing
that you shall regain the powerful energies
of this person
and that s/he shall be renewed
through your unending love.
Let the parting be easy and peaceful.
Let us continue to honor the good works done.
Let us be strong in remembering him/her
by carrying on the memories.
Through these shall s/he live on
in our hearts.
A peaceful journey to you, my friend.

Funeral

Mother of us all,
open your liquid arms wide
and accept this soul
as s/he crosses over the river of life
and returns to you.
Let us not impede the journey.
Instead, let us offer our blessings.
Show him/her the way back to your boundless love and beauty.
Enfold him/her in your affection as we loved him/her.
Show him/her how to rest and then how to become
once again one in the eternal Spirit of all beings
until such time as s/he is ready to return
and become the sacred Child once more.

Memorial

O Great Goddess of everlasting and transcending love,
we honor all those who have gone before us
but, today, we especially wish to honor the life of _____.
Teach us to bless his/her passing of as s/he is returned to you.
Let us be reminded that s/he will be taken into your arms
and comforted.
Let us be reminded that s/he will be returned
to the great joy and beauty of eternal Spirit.
O Great God of wisdom and light,
we honor all those who have gone before us
but, today, we especially wish to honor the life of _____.
teach us to be strong and wise as we remember her/him.
Let us be reminded that as you are reborn again and again,
so shall the spirit of her/him be reborn
and in the name of the Child which is the mystery of life
let us bless the memory of _____
and honor the cycle of life of which we are all a part.

Vow of Dedication

I hereby accept the responsibilities inherent
in seeking a higher level of study by helping others
both within and beyond this circle
and by seeking help when it is needed.
As a seeker of this path, I vow:
> to honor this and all spiritual teachings.
> to respect and honor all practitioners;
> I now know or may know of this and all sacred paths; and
> to respect and honor myself as a unique and sacred being.
I hereby proudly and without reservation,
dedicate myself to becoming a Pagan practitioner.
From this day hence, I proclaim that I am Pagan.

Dewdrops In The Moonlight

Chapter Four

Prayers For Healing

Some of the most powerful work that can be done for the self, for others, and for the Earth is healing work. There can be no ill intent in helping another return to health as long as the cycles of life are respected.

Healing I

Divulge the cold, return (release) the warm.
Return this body to its norm.
Relieve the hurt, relieve the pain.
Return this body to health again.

Healing II

O great God and Goddess,
energy and fullness of life,
we know that you possess the understanding
of the cycles of life.
Only you know when the wheel may turn.
Only you know what lessons need to be learned.
If it is to be that this person needs to gain wisdom through suffering,
help us to guide that person to truth.
If it is to be that this person can be healed,
help us to aid him/her to health.
If it is to be that this person has reached a new stage
in the cycle of life,
help us to ease his/her transition.
Give us the strength, wisdom, and guidance to do what is needed
so that we may all continue to praise and honor you in joy
within this life and beyond.

Healing III

O great and beautiful God of Light,
O bright and bountiful Goddess of Love,
O sacred mysterious Child of Life,
We call upon you.
We ask that the energies of those divine and human
spirits gathered here
Fill this sacred space of loving compassion.
Let the strength that is our common love
Join from the many to the one.
We know that we hurt,
But in communion, we can share the hurt.
We know that we grieve,
But in communion, we can share the grief.
Through the light of the God, we gather strength.
Through the love of the Goddess, we share our compassion.
Through the strength of all those here gathered, we share hope.

Healing for the Self

O great God
give me the strength
to fight this illness.
O great Goddess
give me the compassion
to heal my body.
O Great Child
let me take rest and comfort
so that I may regain my health.
For only through your strength and love
may I be whole again
and, by being whole, will once again
be able to aid you in healing and caring for others.

Healing For the Earth

Goddess of the Earth,
you have been neglected for so long.
Too many years have we believed
that we were given dominion over your children;
that we were made masters of your soil.
Through kind, loving, and gentle patience
you have taught us the truth.
Let us now be as loving, caring, and patient
to your creatures and to you our mother.
Let us find ways to heal the years of pain and abuse
inflicted upon you.
Let us find ways to seek harmony and not destruction.
Let us find ways to sustain you and ourselves.
Most of all, let us learn ways to emulate
and not dominate
your ways of wisdom
your ways of caring
your ways of nurturing for all beings.

Healing For Animals

O eternal gods,
I call to you to heal this animal.
As all creatures are equally the children of the gods,
I ask you to watch over this creature.
Lord, give it the strength it needs to stay healthy and strong.
Lady, fill it with the energies of love and healing.
Let it, like all your children, fulfill its purpose on this earth.

World Peace

O gods of all nations and all peoples, unite!
Show your people that the essence of
all that is truly spiritual is to live life to its fullest;
that what is true for one people is true for all;
that it is our duty as spiritual people
to encourage peace for all;
that to live between the fullness of love
and the emptiness of contentment is to live in peace.
For only in peace can we praise and worship.
God of light reveal to us this truth within us.
Goddess of love, show us how to live together.
Child of life, give us the courage to live in peace
now and forever.

To End Oppression

O Great Gods,
you have taught us to learn through Nature,
you have taught us to love openly and fully,
you have taught us to live with joy,
you have taught us to seek truth in all places.
You have taught us these things:
that learning, living, and loving can not be experienced
if one is hungry, oppressed, poor, or ignored;
that they who are discriminated against
cannot laugh or sing or dance
in the sacred circle of life;
that life is the gift of all beings everywhere;
that love is the blessing of all beings everywhere; and
that light is the chance for growth for all beings everywhere.
Let us find ways to help those in need.
Let us find ways to lift the downtrodden.
Let us find ways to feed the hungry.
Let us find ways to seek justice for the oppressed.
For it is right that all creatures be given the chance
to live in the joys of life
that are the gifts of the bountiful gods.

Blessings

With these prayers, we offer blessings upon ourselves and others. A blessing is a way of recognizing the value of another. In effect, you are saying that someone or something is worth the consideration of the gods to be honored. It is similar to offering a prayer for health except that one need not already be sick. Instead, you are asking that one be continuously bestowed with strong health and good fortune.

General Blessing I

Blessed with eternal joy are you
who knows the sacred mysteries;
who lives the sanctified life;
joins all in mystic unity
and, by these rites, is made whole.
Blessed are you who
enters the ecstasy of the silent mountain,
knows the peace of calm breezes,
shines with the brightness of a single flame,
and is filled with the happiness of running rivers.
Blessed are you who knows
the turning of the moon, sun, and stars
in the great wheel of life.
You, who observes these cycles in your rites
made of the Great Mother,
blessed by the Great Father, and
fulfilled by the Great Child,
shall be forever blessed.

General Blessing II

May your mind know wisdom.
May your heart find love.
May your soul embrace peace.
And may the work of your hands
be blessed and bless others
all the days of your life.

General Blessing III

May the earth hold you;
may the winds protect you;
may the sun give you warmth
and the river guide you;
and may the path be walked in peace;
may we always live in peace.

Blessing for a Non-Pagan

O God of light,
bless this person
who may not walk my path
but who is also full of your light.
O Goddess of love,
bless this person
who may not walk my path
but who is also worthy of love.
O Child of Life,
bless this person
who may not walk my path
but who is a blessing to life.
For I know that all paths
which cause no harm
may lead to truth.
I respect the paths of others
so they may respect mine.
I honor the lives of others
so they may honor mine.
for when I say:
"as it harm none, do as you will,"
I say it for all.

Parents

O Lord and Lady,
as you have been the strong and proud parents of all,
Show us how to do the same.
You have showered love and understanding upon your children.
Show us how to do the same.
You have taught your children how to seek truth.
Show us how to do the same.
You have been a trusted friend and companion to your children.
Show us how to do the same.
You have been there always for your children.
Show us how to do the same.

Pets

O great ancient Ones,
as all creatures are equally a part of creation,
and as are all your blessed children,
I ask that you watch over my pets.
Guide them and protect them.
Teach me to love and honor them as they do me
and as I do you.
for the love of all things at all times is divine.

Animals

From the teachings of the God we learn
that all life is sacred,
not just our own.
The lives of all creatures are sacred
for we are all blessed with the same spark
of the divine.
From the teachings of the Goddess we learn
that all is love
and that the unconditional love for all life
is the greatest energy of the universe.
O great Gods,
teach us to love, honor, and respect all creatures
as sacred beings.
We ask that you bless these creatures,
offer them protection in their lives
and grant us the knowledge and the means
to keep them safe and happy.

Meals I

Ancient mother of us all,
we join together here in peace at this table of fellowship
to honor you and thank you for these blessed gifts of food.
From you we receive and to you we return.
Let this act of eating and all acts in your name be sacred.

Meals II

O Ancient Ones,
you are the beginning and ending
of the eternal cycles.
As we prepare to partake of this food
we, too, become part of the cycle
of death and rebirth.
We offer thanks to you for these gifts
which shall nourish us
and through which
we may continue to honor you
with good works.
For all acts of good and right
done in love
are the manifestations
of your presence.

Meals III

O Mother Earth, Goddess Gaia,
from you we receive and to you we return.
May we receive in gratitude and moderation
these gifts of food and all the gifts of the day
and may we return that gratitude through our good works.

House

O Ancient Gods of many names,
Fill this house with your presence of goodness and beauty.
Let each room be filled with joy and happiness.
Let all those who enter be filled with this divine energy.
Let none enter who wish to cause harm.
O Great Ones,
bless this house and all who pass within it
for now and for all the days to come.
This we ask in humble praise.

Garden

O Lady.
though I set the garden,
it is from you that the plants must come.
O Lord,
though I plant the seeds,
it is through your light that they grow.
These things I recognize:
that through my work
and with your blessing,
these plants shall take root and grow.
I marvel at the miracle in which I take part.

For The Earth

The breath of the earth is my breath.
The strength of the earth is my strength.
The soul of the earth is my soul
My body comes from the body of the earth.
My thoughts come from her wisdom.
My love comes from the love of her creatures.
The life of the earth am I.
May I live to bless her
as she has blessed my life.

Ritual Water

Water is life giving, life sustaining, and life renewing.
It makes up the majority of the surface of the planet
as well as the majority of the materials of our bodies.
It is a symbol of the Spiritual.
We are like drops of water -
like rain that falls from above.
Seemingly separate, we often do not realize
that we are part of a greater reality.
As we observe how raindrops collect to form streams,
how streams become rivers and then mighty oceans
teeming with other life,
we begin to understand the connections between all life.
Water is the drink of life and a reflection of the spiritual.
In the ripples of moving waters, we see the face of the Goddess.
O Ancient Gods, bless this water we offer here for our coming rituals
and work.
Let it constantly remind us of the blessings of life and of our
connection to all living things.
Let it be used for good and right, for beauty and truth,
and for growth and nurturance in our sacred work.

Tool Blessing

Blessings will this [tool]bestow
Upon those who come to know
That good tidings shall be enjoyed
When with good intention employed.
But if thy Will seeks sorrow or pain
Then with this tool shall ye reap no gain
And thus shall thy graft return like thunder
To cause this [tool] to be rent asunder!

Candle

Gods of many names and many places
but of all one eternity,
bless this candle.
Let it stand tall to support my intent.
Let is burn bright and steady to carry my hopes
and if my intent is good and true,
let the flame send out that intent into the universe
and carry out the work for which it is meant
for I know that its light and my light
come from the same source of light.
Its heat is the same as the heat within my body.
Its incense fills the air as does my breath.
Let us work together as one.

The Altar

Sacred altar, realm of visions, symbol of the integrated being;
the ground beneath my feet,
accept and support the weight of my intent.
Prepare the way for good works and offerings
upon this blessed altar.

Tarot Invocation

Let by these cards, knowledge gained.
That which needs must be attained.
Reveal here what we need to know
and to all good this truth bestow.

Tarot Evocation

And now this work shall see an end,
let no harm from it append.
All energies here to good I send
and let these truths neither harm nor offend.

Prayers for Teaching

Teaching is as much an act of magick as any ritual. Teachers must take the raw material of the student and transform him or her into a shiny polished diamond - able to reflect the best of what Paganism can offer to themselves and the community. Within this section are offered prayers for beginning and ending class sessions. Following them, I offer brief readings that I have adapted from the wisdom and sacred texts of the world's religions which, in my opinion, reflect the essence of that teaching. They can be used in celebrations of world religions or in classes in which these religions may be a topic for discussion.

Class Opening

From the East, may we come to grow in wisdom.
From the South, may we come to grow in joy,
From the West may we come to be grow through Spirit.
From the North may we come to grow in support of one another.
And from the center may we remember that learning the Mysterious
is a life long journey. Welcome and Blessed Be!

Class Closing

From the Center where the journey begins and ends
From the North which is the earth and our body.
From the West which is the water and our blood.
From the South which is the fire that keeps us warm.
And from the East which is the wind and the air we breath,
may we know that we are all connected as one.
Merry Meet, Merry Part, and Merry Meet again
Blessed Be!

Prayer For A Teacher

O Ancient and Wise Gods,
you have taught me well.
You have given me glimpses of truth
and a path to pursue them.
You have given more powerful words
and the chance to absorb them.
You have sent me wise teachers
and the patience to hear them.
You have shown me ways in which to develop
and have waited for me to grow.
You have shown me how use my gifts to reach out
and have helped me to help others.
Show me now how to be
as wise, caring, nurturing and helpful
to those who wish to learn
and carry on the good works
in your name.

Prayer For A Student

O Lady of Love,
touch this student
so that s/he may know love
and pass on your gifts to others.
O Lord of Light,
touch this student
so that s/he may be enlightened
and pass on your gifts to others.
O Child of Life,
fill this student
so that s/he full
of the joy of living
and pass on this gift to others.
O Great Teachers of the Old Ways,
enrich this student with your blessings.
Open the mind, open the heart,
fill the soul, and strengthen the body.
Give him/her what s/he needs to grow in wisdom
and become a living example of your truth.

Hindu Prayer

Whosoever sees the spiritual in all there is knows the truth and knows
this most of all: That which is of all things is also of the self.
Whosoever knows the self is spiritual cannot harm the self nor the self
in others and, therefore, walks the higher path.
(adapted rom the Bhagavad Gita)

Taoist Prayer

The way to live life is not to resist life. The way to live life is just to
be. When one knows this all becomes clear and the desire to go astray
is abandoned by simple truth. When one lives this way then life is
filled with joy. When one lives this way then life is filled with peace.
(adapted from the Tao Te Ching #37)

Christian Prayer

God is love; love is everywhere.
God is love; and he who dwells in love dwells in God. Before there was one called I, there was love that forever was and forever shall be. We are created from love and from love is derived all righteous living. From love we come; from love we grow; and to love we return.
(adapted ffrom the Gospel of John 4:16 and the writings of Julian of Norwich)

Muslim Prayer

By the sun and its brightness; by the moon that follows it;
by the day and its splendor; by the night which veils it.
By the heavens and that which caused them;
by the earth and that which brought it;
by the soul and that which molded it and inspired it.
Blessed are those that keep these things sacred
and surrender to the will of that which made them.
(adapted from the Koran - 91:1)

Jewish Prayer

Search for wisdom as you would silver.
Search for wisdom as you would hidden treasure.
Though silver is spent, wisdom remains.
Gain wisdom and in all you seek, seek understanding.
Thus these things will guide you and protect you for all of your days.
(adapted from the Book of Proverbs – 2)

Confucian Prayer

If one can be respectful, then one can gain respect.
If one can be tolerant then one will know great people.
Seek to be virtuous.
The one that can be trusted will earn great honor.
The one that is devoted will earn great rewards.
Seek to be virtuous.
The one that learns to commit one's self to the task at hand
will do great things.
Seek to be virtuous.
(adapted from the Analects of Confucius - xv.6)

Buddhist Prayer

As weeds go unchecked in the field,
so desires grow wildly and cause suffering.
Uproot these weeds and manage them through wisdom.
Thus the fields shall be free
and sorrow shall be like rain that falls from shining leaves.
(adapted from the Dhammapada - 24)

Invocations To Deity

Many people recite the traditional Charge of the Goddess in their rites. I offer here an alternative form of the traditional Charge with these Calls to the main deities. Each points out correspondences including the seasonal event, the gender quality, and the tools associated with the particular deity - including Spirit. I have also included a deity concept from my tradition which has not been practiced by many - the Child. The Child is the life principle - the manifestation of the forces of God and Goddess. Without the divine parents, there is no child and without the child, there can be no parents. This deity is celebrated at the Astor or dark of the moon when the stars in the night sky are most visible.

The Call of the Goddess

Hear the call of the Goddess:
Come together, O followers of the Lady.
Gather round when you are ready
During the nights when the moon is full -
Hear my sacred call to you.
Dance and sing all in my name.
Make love and music all the same;
For I am the essence of femininity.
Joining in love is my affinity.
I am the love that binds all things.
I am the song the lover sings.
Mine is the chalice of the water of life
Whose truth washes clean all fear and strife.
Mine is the earth in all its forms.
I am the calm seas as well as the storms.
Let none stop you once you begin
To seek joyous union here and again;
For all these things shall you live and learn
And then to me shall you return.

The Call of the God

Here the call of the God:
Come together, O followers of the Lord.
Gather round by staff and sword
During the days when the great sun burns
That mark the seasons when the Great Wheel turns.
You shall gather as the ancients do
To learn my sacred call to you.
Let your bodies bask in my heat.
Make glad your hearts and merry meet;
For I am the essence of masculinity.
Growth in the light is my affinity.
I am the light within all that lives.
I am the joy that pure love gives.
Mine is the blade that cuts false from true;
Pointing the way for the light to shine through.
Mine is the flame of the dancing fire.
I am the heart that burns with desire.
Let none stop you from shining bright.
Let one and all bring forth inner light.
For all these things shall you live and know
And come through me to fully grow.

The Call of the Child

Hear the call of the Child:
Come together, O followers of the Child.
Gather round without want or wile.
During the nights when the dark moon is neigh.
When the stars shine bright within the sky.
You shall let love and trust ensue
As you hear my call to you.
Enjoy in full measure the life you lead.
Take full well this gift of life decreed;
For I am the essence of sacred mystery.
The dance of life is my affinity.
I am revealed in the unraveled fear
Like the twinkle of stars that in dark appear.
Mine is the silence from which all sound begins.
I am that which never begins nor ends.
Mine is the center of the turning wheel –
The inner essence that is forever still.
Let none stop you from seeking silence.
Let none sway you from inner guidance.
So long as harm shall not be sent
Live through me in full intent.

The Call of Spirit

In the name of Spirit,
which is of all and of nothing,
and yet is greater,
which is neither beginning nor end
and yet is greater,
which is neither male nor female
and yet is greater,
which is neither mortal nor immortal
and yet is greater,
which is neither above or below nor within or without
and yet is greater,
which is all of these things and more

and less,
we come together.

In the name of Spirit,
the sum of all consciousness and mystery,
the essence of all spiritual insight,
the wellspring of all creativity,
the source of all energy and knowing,
the fount of all love, light, and life eternal,
the apex of the elements,
the eternal oneness and void,
we come together.

In the name of Spirit:
the ineffable, the incomprehensible, the immutable,
the incomparable, the inexpressible, the inconceivable,
we come together.

We gather not so much to worship
as to honor.
We gather not so much to praise
as to learn.
We gather not so much to be filled
as to fulfill.
We gather not so much to learn to accept
as to learn to give.

In the name of that which has so many names
but is truly without name,
we come together.

For the Goddess at the Esbat

O Mother Moon, Goddess entity,
the source of femininity,
hear my words addressed to thee.
I come before thee most reverently.
In you I celebrate the receiving-
to accept what is true and nurturing.
In you I celebrate gentle intuition-
the will to trust the unclear vision.
And now I this candle light
to honor you this sacred night.

For the God at the Sabbat

O Father Sun, God entity,
the source of masculinity.
Hear my words addressed to thee.
I come before thee most reverently.
In you I celebrate the selfless giving-
To offer what I can to all those living.
In you I celebrate strength and courage-
the work that makes all grow and flourish.
And now this candle light's display
will be to honor you this sacred day.

For the Child at the Astor

O Child Star, mysterious entity,
the source and subject of creativity,
hear my words addressed to thee.
I come before thee most reverently.
In you I celebrate the unbegun-
the good work yet to be done.
In you I celebrate the great return-
the unity of love we have yet to learn.
And now I this candle light
to honor you this sacred night

Litany for the Goddess

O great Goddess,
come to us.
Mother of us all,
come to us.
Blessed Mother of the Earth,
come to us.
She, whose face shines in the silver moon,
come to us.
She, who wraps us in her arms of love,
come to us.
Like a flower that opens its petals to the air,
come to us.
Like the water that flows through deep forests,
come to us.
Join us now, O sweet Lady,
come to us.

Litany for the God

O Great God,
come to us.
Father of us all,
come to us.
Blessed Father of the sky,
come to us.
He, whose face shines in the golden sun,
come to us.
He, who fills us with sacred light.
come to us.
Like the warm breeze that fills us,
come to us.
Like the fire that warms and protects us,
come to us.
Join us now, O great Lord,
come to us.

Litany for the Child

O sacred Child,
let us be present.
Mystery of all,
let us be present.
Great miracle of creation,
let us be present.
You, whose face shines in the starlit heavens,
let us be present.
You, who gives us the strength of life,
let us be present.
Like the silence that stills us,
let us be present.
Like the center of the wheel,
let us be present.
With you, O great force of the universe,
let us be present.

Mantras

These mantras are offered for silent introspective prayer or for meditation work. Mantras depend on the vibratory energy of the words, whether spoken aloud or silently, to still the mind and open up the deep inner recesses of the self. The wheel of life spins madly about us but we can choose to focus on the center of the wheel, where it is silent and the motion is slow, to center our own lives. It is from this center that we grow and learn. Some mantras depend on the actual sounds of the words or of the consonants within to set up this vibration. The most famous mantra is the use of the word "OM." With this sound, we hear an open O sound close off to a humming M sound. We gather ourselves from the open spaces and move into the central vibratory sound of the M. Try humming and feel how that sound sends vibrations through your whole body. By focusing on certain sounds and phrases, we can attune to these vibrations and open ourselves up. Work with these mantras by repeating them to yourself continuously until you get past these words and feel only the sounds. Let your mind become still and focused and open your heart so that it becomes receptive. Let these words gently massage your soul.

In Air and Fire, ever higher.
In Water and Stone, fully known.

I am Light, I am Love, I am Life.

To learn to love to live in light and laughter.

Come my Lord, come my Lady, come.

Within this spinning spiral, this is the silent center.

Lord of Light, Lady of Love, I am your messenger, I am your song.

Truth and right, beauty and light, fill me!

Home, my mother, home!

Through truth and light, greater insight.
Through below and above, greater love.

I, the empty vessel, fill me!

Open slowly, grow fully, now.

Fear not the silence,
Fear not the dark,
Fear not the mystery!

Ah! Father of all!

Great Goddess, thy love is boundless!

Guide us, protect us, love us!

We are thou and thou art we.

Precious petal by precious petal, the flower opens. Praise her!

In this sacred space,
my mind is clear,
my heart is open,
my soul is blessed.

All future, all past
all beginnings, all endings, now!

Whole and holy only you.

Prayer Endings

The following is a collection of prayer endings which can be used as the final statement for all prayers. This simple ending phrase can do many powerful things. It assures that your prayer is meant for good and right not just for yourself but for all beings. It assures that you are asking for something not just for your own personal worldly gain. It assures that any evil or mistaken intent in a prayer will be lost. By ending a prayer with an appropriate final phrase, you send that prayer off with a blessing of righteousness for the intent cannot take place unless it meets the requirement of the demand listed at the end of the prayer.

For the good of one and all, so mote it be.

For now and forever in your name.

So it is sent. So it shall be. So it shall return.

Amen, Amain, Namaste, Blessed be.

By Earth, Air, Fire, Water and Spirit eternal, so mote it be.

In Light, Life, and Love now and forever.

In the service of goodness, truth, and beauty, so it shall be.

Blessed be this work. Blessed be what shall come of it. Blessed be those lives touched by it.

As above, so below. As within, so without. As in thought, so in action.

With these words to the wisdom of the universe, so be it.

In your mind, in your hearts, in your soul and through your works, make it so.

Dewdrops In The Moonlight

Appendix

Pantheons

The following is a list of pantheons or groupings of gods and goddesses of several different cultures. I strongly recommend that you find out as much about a god or goddess before invoking him or her. Each has been invoked by thousands of people and their names carry the energies of those many invocations. If you feel a connection with any of these pantheons or particular deities, their name can be easily inserted into the prayers above.

Aztec Gods

Acat	God of life.
Chalchihuitilicue	Goddess of storms, beauty, spring growth, love, flowers, spirits.
Chantico	Goddess of fire, home and fertility,
Chicomecoatl	Maize (corn) goddess.
Cihuacoatl	Goddess of childbirth.
Cinteotl	God of corn.
Coatlicue	Earth goddess.
Coyolxauhqui	Moon goddess.
Ueuecoyotl	Trickster god.
Huehueteotl	God of fire
Huitzilopochtli	God of the sun, death, war, young men, warriors, storms.
Ilamatecuhtli	Mother goddess.
Itzcoliuhqui	God of darkness, terrible cold, volcanic eruptions, and disaster
Itzpaplotl	Goddess of fate, stars, and agriculture.
Mayauel	Goddess of women in childbirth.
Mictlantecuhtli	God of the underworld and the North.
Mixcoatl	God of the pole star
Quetzalcoatl	God of the wind, sea breeze, and life breath.
Tezcatlipoca	God of warriors, magicians and divination.
Tlaloc	God of mountains, rains, hail, fertility, water, clouds, thunder, and lightning.
Tlazolteotl	Goddess of the earth and witches.

Tonatiuh	Sun god; ruler of fate.
Tozi/Teteoinnan	Goddess of healing.
Xipe Totec	God of agriculture.
Xochipilli	God of music, dance, and ball players.
Xochiquetzal	Goddess of the underworld and flowers.
Yacatecuhtli	God of merchants and traders.

Celtic Gods
(the Tuatha Dé Danann)

Dagda	The all father.
Danu	Mother goddess. Earth goddess of plenty.
Badb	Goddess of war.
Aine	Goddess of the hidden paths in the realms of the Western ocean.
Aonghus	God of Youth
Banbha	The goddess of sovereignty.
Brigit	Goddess of culture and poetry.
Lugh	Sun god and a hero god.
Ler	God of the sea.
Cernunnos	God of nature, virility, fertility, and animals.
Ogma	The god of wisdom.

Chinese Gods

Ao	The Four dragon kings. Gods of rain and the sea.
Ch'ang-o/Heng-o	Goddess of the Moon.
Ch'eng-Huang	God of walls and ditches.
Chih-Nii/Chih Nu	Goddess of spinners, weavers and clouds.
Ch'in-Shu-Pao	Guardian god.
Chuang-Mu	Goddess of the sexual delights.
Chu-Jung	God of fire and executions.
Erh-Lang	God who chases away evil spirits.
Feng-Po-Po	Goddess of winds.
Fu-Hsi/Fu-Hsing	God of happiness.
Hou-Chi	Harvest god.
Hsuan-T'ien-Shang-Ti	God of exorcism.

Hu-Tu/Hou-T'u	Earth goddess
I-Ti	God of wine.
Kuan Ti	God of war and fortunetelling.
Kuan Yin/Kwan Yin	Great Mother; goddess of compassion and mercy.
K'uei-Hsing	God of tests and examinations, literature, and students.
Lan Ts'ai-Ho	Goddess of music.
Lao-Tien-Yeh	The Jade Emperor; great god.
Lei-King/Lei-Kung	God of thunder and retribution.
Lo-Shen	Goddess of rivers.
Lu-Hsing	God of salaries and employees .
Ma-Ku	Goddess of spring time.
Nu Kua	Creator Goddess.
Pa	Goddess of droughts
P'an Chin Lien	Goddess of Prostitutes.
Pi-Hsia Yuan Chin	Goddess of childbirth and labor.
Sao-Ts'ing Niang	Goddess of the clouds.
Shang-Ti	The supreme god.
Shen Nung	God of medicine, pharmacy, and agriculture.
Shou Hsing	God of longevity.
Shui-Khan	God of protection.
T'ai-Yueh- Ta-Ti	God of the affairs of men.
T'ien Khuan	God who bestows happiness.
Tien-Mu	Goddess of lighting
Ti-Khuan	God who grants remission of sins.
Ti-Tsang	God of mercy.
Tou-Mou	Goddess of the polestar and record keeper.
Tsai hen	God of wealth.
Tsao Wang	God of the hearth.
Twen-Ch'ang	God of literature and poetry.

Egyptian Gods

Ammut	Goddess of the gate of the underworld.
Anqet	Water goddess.
Bastet	Goddess of Fire, cats , and pregnant women.
Hathor	Goddess of love, happiness, dance and music.

Isis	Goddess of life and death.
Ma'at	Goddess of the physical and moral law of Egypt.
Mut	Great mother goddess.
Nut	Goddess of the daytime sky.
Qetesh	Nature goddess
Satet	Goddess of fertility.
Sekhmet	Goddess of war and destruction.
Selket	Goddess of scorpions and magick.
Tefnut	Goddess of rain
Amon	Creator god.
Anubis	God of mummification.
Bes	God of music and dance.
Geb	God of the Earth.
Hapi	God of the Nile.
Horus	The Falcon headed god.
Khensu	Moon god.
Khnemu	Water god and protector.
Min	God of the generative force of nature.
Osiris	God of the Earth and Vegetation.
Ra	The sun god of Annu.
Seth	God of deserts and storms.
Shu	God of the space and light between the sky and the earth.
Sobek	God of sacred animals.
Thoth	God of wisdom and learning.

Finnish Gods

Ahto/Ahti	Chief god of waters and seas.
Rauni	Goddess of the harvest and female sexuality.
Hiisi	God of evil, sorcerers, and necromancers.
Ilma	God of the air.
Ilmatar	Creatress goddess.
Ilmarinen	God of smiths, magick, and prosperity.
Jumala/Mader-Atcha	Supreme creator god.
Kalma	Goddess of death.
Kipu-Tytto	Goddess of illness.
Kuu	Moon goddess

Leib-Olmai	Laplander bear god.
Louhi	Goddess of sorcery, evil, dark magick.
Loviator	Goddess of plagues and evil.
Mielikki	Goddess of the Forest.
Num	A Samoyed sky god.
Numitorem	A Vogul sky god who created all animals.
Paiva	Sun God.
Pellervoinen	God of fields.
Rauni	Thunder goddess.
Tapio	God of water and woods.
Tuoni	God of the underworld
Vammatar	God of death.
Ukko	Supreme god.

Greek Gods

Aphrodite	Goddess of love, beauty and fertility.
Apollo	God of prophecy, archery and music.
Ares	War god.
Artemis	Virgin goddess of the wild.
Asclepius	God of healing.
Athena	Virgin goddess of war and crafts.
Demeter	Goddess of vegetation, fruitfulness, and the earth.
Dionysus	God of vegetation, wine and ecstasy.
Eos	Winged goddess of dawn.
Eros	God of love
Hades	God of the underworld.
Hecate	Goddess of farming, witchcraft, ghosts, and tombs.
Helios	Sun god.
Hephaistos	Smith god.
Hera	Supreme goddess.
Hermes	Messenger god.
Hestia	Goddess of hearth
Pan	God of mountainsides and pastures.
Poseidon	Sea god.
Selene	Moon goddess.

Silenus	God of pastures.
Zeus	Supreme god.

Hawaiian Gods

Keawe	Creator god.
Kane or eli-eli	God of natural phenomena.
Ku	God of war, woodlands and crops, and craftsmen.
Kuhuluhulumanu	God and bird catchers and feather workers.
Ku'ula	God of fishermen.
Kukoae	God of sorcerers.
Kanaloa	God of seamen
Lono	God of medicine.
Laka	Goddess of hula
Kapo	Goddess of the South Pacific

Japanese Gods

Ama No Uzume	Fertility goddess.
Amaterasu	Sun goddess.
Amida	The Buddha of Infinite Light.
Benten	Goddess of good luck.
Chimati no Kami	God of crossroads and footpaths.
Fugen Bosatsu	God of enlightening wisdom, intelligence, and understanding.
Haya-Ji	God of the winds and whirlwind.
Inari	Goddess of rice.
Ishikore-Dome	Goddess of the mirror.
Izanagi	Creator god and earth god
Kannon Bosatsu	God of mercy and compassion
Kaya Nu Hima	Goddess of Herbs
Nai No Kami	God of earthquakes.
Naru Kami	Goddess of thunder.
O-Kuni-Nushi	Earth god.
O-Ryu	Goddess of the willow tree.
O-Wata-Tsumi	God of the tides and the sea creatures.
O-Yama_Tsu-Mi	God of all mountains and volcanoes.

Rafu-Sen	Goddess of the plum blossoms
Sakyamuni	Japanese name for the Buddha.
Susanoo	God of storm and thunder.
Toyota Mahime	Sea goddess
Uso Dori	Goddess of singing.

Mayan Gods

Acat	God of life.
Ahpuch	God of death.
Bacabs	Gods of the four winds and the four directions.
Chac	Rain and vegetation god.
Ek Ahau	War god
Gucumatz	God of agriculture and civilization.
Hunab Ku	Supreme god.
Hurukan	God who created Earth, animals, fire and people.
Itzamna	Sky god; father of the gods and creator of humankind.
Ixchebelyax	Goddess of painting and designing.
Ixcehl	Goddess of childbirth.
Ixchup	Moon goddess
Kukulcan	God of light, learning, and culture.
Mam	Earthquake god of Yucatan.
Masaya	Goddess of volcanoes and divination.
Nohochacyum	God of creation.
Yum Caax	God of maize or corn.

Native American Gods

Agloolik	Eskimo god of hunters and fishermen.
Aipaloovik	Eskimo god of vandalism and destruction.
Asagaya Gigaei	Thunder god of the Cherokees
Ataentsic	Iroquois/Huron goddess of marriage, childbirth, feminine crafts.
Atius Tirawa	Pawnee creator god.
Aulanerk	Eskimo god of the tides and waves.
Coyote	A trickster god.
Estsanatlehi	Navajo goddess of immortality.

Hahbwehdiyu	Iroquois creator god
Igtinike	Lakota war god.
Innua	Eskimo supreme god.
Iyatiku	Pueblo corn goddess.
Manitou	Supreme god.
Michabo	Algonquin creator of Earth and animals.
Nokomis	Algonquin Earth goddess.
Onatha	Iroquois goddess of wheat and harvest.
Orenda	Iroquois supreme god.
Pinga	Eskimo goddess of game.
Raven	A Trickster god, similar to Coyote
Sedna	Eskimo goddess of the sea and its creatures.
Shakuru	Pawnee sun god.
Tekkeitsertok	Eskimo god of deer and hunting.
Thunder Bird	Messenger between man and the gods.
Tirawa	Pawnee creator and sky god.
Tonenili	Navajo rain god
Panthers	Evil gods of water but a source of great wisdom and healing.
Wakan Tanka	Oglala supreme god.
Wakonda	Lakota supreme god.
Yanauluha	Zuni god of civilization, agriculture, animal husbandry, and social life.
Yolkai Estasan	Navajo earth goddess.

Norse Gods

Alaisiagae	War goddess
Freyja	Goddess of great power and magickal knowledge.
Frigg	Goddess of childbirth, physical love, wisdom, and magick.
Gullveig	Goddess of magick, foreseeing, prophecy, and healing
Hel	Goddess of the underworld, dark magick, revenge, and rebirth.
Idhunn	Goddess of long life.
Nanna	Earth goddess.

Nerthus	Goddess of peace, fertility, witchcraft, wealth, the sea, and purification.
Ran	Goddess of the sea, sailors, and storms
Stiff	Goddess of harvest, fruitfulness, plenty and generosity.
Sjofna	Goddess of love
Odin	The all father.
Thor	God of the common man.
Loki	Trickster god.
Tyr	Sky god.
Ull	God of the bow and the snowshoe.

Roman Gods

Aurora	Goddess of the dawn.
Bacchus	God of wine.
Ceres	Goddess of the earth, vegetation and fruitfulness.
Cupid	Love god.
Diana	Virgin goddess of hunting and light
Eileithyia	Goddess of birth.
Funus	God of mountainsides.
Flora	Goddess of spring and flowering plants.
Janus	God of beginnings and endings.
Juno	Queen of the sky.
Jupiter	Supreme sky god.
Mars	God of spring and war.
Mercury	Messenger god.
Minerva	Goddess of wisdom and the arts.
Neptune	Sea god.
Saturn	Corn god and father of time.
Sol	Sun god.
Venus	Goddess of love.
Vesta	Goddess of the hearth.
Vulcan	Smith god.

Welsh Gods

Arianrhod	Star goddess of time and karma.
Cerridwen	Goddess of nature.
Cernunnos	God of nature, virility, fertility, and animals.
Hu Gadarn	God of the underworld and astral planes.
Morrighan	Goddess of magick.

Printed in the USA
CPSIA information can be obtained
at www.ICGtesting.com
LVHW041756120923
757983LV00003B/106

9 780615 144979